CAT PSALMS

Cat Psalms

Prayers and Spiritual Lessons from Our Beloved Companions

HERBERT BROKERING

BROADLEAF BOOKS
Minneapolis

CAT PSALMS

Prayers and Spiritual Lessons from Our Beloved Companions

Copyright © 2003 Herbert Brokering. First Broadleaf Books edition published 2024. Published by Broadleaf Books, an imprint of 1517 Media. All rights reserved. Except for brief quotations in critical articles or reviews, no part of this book may be reproduced in any manner without prior written permission from the publisher. Email copyright@1517.media or write to Permissions, Broadleaf Books, PO Box 1209, Minneapolis, MN 55440-1209.

Library of Congress Cataloging-in-Publication Data

Names: Brokering, Herbert, 1926-2009, author.
Title: Cat psalms : prayers my cats have taught me / Herbert Brokering.
Description: First Broadleaf Books edition. | Minneapolis : Broadleaf
   Books, 2024.
Identifiers: LCCN 2023022869 (print) | LCCN 2023022870 (ebook) | ISBN
   9781506494449 (hardback) | ISBN 9781506499277 (ebook)
Subjects: LCSH: Cat owners—Prayers and devotions. | Cats—Religious
   aspects—Christianity.
Classification: LCC BV4596.A54 B76 2024 (print) | LCC BV4596.A54 (ebook)
   | DDC 242.2—dc23/eng/20230906
LC record available at https://lccn.loc.gov/2023022869
LC ebook record available at https://lccn.loc.gov/2023022870

Cover Design: Jim Terney

Print ISBN: 978-1-5064-9444-9
eBook ISBN: 978-1-5064-9927-7

Dedicated to my son Chris,
who helped kittens grow into good cats,
and to cats who have helped me pray:

Peveley

Kitty Black

Tinkie

Petsy

Tiger

Tiger II

Teewee

Machant

Dudley

Buffey

Alex

Tetra

Contents

1
Introduction
Cats help me pray

I LEARN FROM metaphors: I look at one thing and understand another thing in myself. I am like a lily of the field, a sower who went out to sow, a wind in trees, bread broken, a mustard seed.

Most often, I am like the cat.

In cats, I see images of myself, of my soul. I watch a cat at peace, and I feel peace. I see a cat leaping gracefully, and my spirit leaps. *Cat Psalms* is about cats and the spirit. We find meaning in nature and spirit.

Cats have always been part of my life. I do not remember not knowing a cat in my seventy-five years.

I've known farm cats, alley cats, house cats. Mostly I grew up knowing barn cats whose kittens would run and hide if a stranger got near. But they knew us. They took the milk we brought them; they let us touch them, tame them. I was learning about my spirit.

On our Nebraska farm, we came inside when the sun went down. Our cats went outside into the dark, unafraid. I wondered what they knew of the night that I would never see. My spirit, too, wanted to prowl in the dark.

I married a cat lover. On our long honeymoon drive to West Virginia, Lois and I were given a kitten in a Nebraska filling station—our first cat. As it grew up, that cat became a companion for our children—the first of many Cat Brokerings. The cats who lived and died in our home were friends and members of the family.

Our four children made clothes for the cats, built them houses, provided toys, taught them games, cuddled in bed with them on winter nights. The cats told us things about each other and ourselves.

Today our children no longer live with us. Now Lois and I have Alex and Tetra. One is a very white cat, one very black. Tetra peers through long black fur with round yellow eyes as though he has been all places in the universe. He looks wise, sometimes distant, sometimes sulky. In the morning, Tetra waits for the door of the basement to open. Lois opens the door for him. Tetra thinks Lois is God.

Alex stands like a white Egyptian statue, waiting for a morsel and purring. He looks at us and begins to purr. He is sick, and he purrs. He is chastised and soon purrs. Alex is a purring machine.

Tetra and Alex follow us nervously when we pack for a trip. They miss us when we are gone and are glad when we return. From Tetra and Alex, we learn about curiosity, affection, anger, love, awe, contentment, elegance. They show me my spirit, my moods; they show me how I am with my Master.

Cat Psalms is a book about what I learned from cats I have known. *Cat psalms* are prayers of my spirit, my soul. Each psalm expresses an observation about a cat's nature in the voice of the cat, followed by a prayer in which my spirit speaks of its catlike nature to God.

My cats have taught me how to pray more deeply, with more imagination and understanding. This book is for all who seek to deepen their own prayer lives, imaging through nature. May the psalms give you fresh ways to see yourselves and new ways to pray.

Herbert Brokering

Herbert Brokering

I am elegant

I AM PRINCESS. *I am prince.*

See me hold my head high as I walk as though I wear a velvet scarf, a gold necklace, a sapphire bracelet, a crown. They cannot tell I am old. I have heard them guess at my age. For a while, I do not ache. And then I prance and leap. And they guess me young. When they look away, slowly I settle into my basket and curl and snuggle. I breathe through my age and feel good years draw over me like a warm blanket. I am old. I am tired. But when I hold my head high, when I walk with careful grace, they guess me young.

O GOD,

You clothe my soul in fine raiment. Your promises are as soft as silk and precious jewels. I walk with my head high for all to see. I am young though I am old, for your blessings clothe me in elegance. They will see me, if but for a second, as elegant. I will show the gifts of my royal side, and they will know who lies curled quietly, breathing evenly, snuggled inside a royal soul dressed in your likeness.

Listen to me purr

I PURR.

Sometimes they do not hear. Sometimes they stop talking, look my way, smile. They are sure they made me purr. Perhaps they did. I cannot always tell where and why my purring begins. Purring is a sound that comes when I am at home, inside, and don't need to go anywhere else—when I am warm and content. It comes when they pet me and tickle my chin. It is not easy to purr when someone is chasing me or if I am lost or cold or wet. I purr best when someone I know well and trust is with me.

DEAR GOD,

You give my soul a sound of its own, a language not in the dictionary. Its tune cannot be forced or commanded. My soul will sing when it must, when it decides from deep inside. My soul breathes songs and anthems with no words. All my good thoughts are in one sound; they repeat like the refrain of a hymn, a mantra. The peaceful sound of my soul is mine by heart. It stops. I look and listen to find it again. It begins where it left off. My soul purrs at the twinkle of the eye. My soul's purr is a lullaby, a pastel painting, a soft cotton cover. My soul's purr vibrates breath, life, spirit. Dear God, it is so when I let you rock my soul.

I have many moods

I AM CAT. *I have many moods.*

I show all feelings, all emotions. My moods shift from moment to moment. Sometimes I am not easy to love and will not be held. When they call, I do not hear and will not turn my head to them. Sometimes I will close my eyes and do not notice. Sometimes I will hiss or snap. When I choose, I will come to the ones I know and be loved by them. Then I show my great emotion, my love: I hold the one holding me. We will not let each other go until I decide to leave. To those I trust, I will return to lie at their feet. Again, I will be held, and I will hold.

O GOD,

My soul is a pendulum, swinging from dark to light to dusk to dawn. I go in all directions. I come, and I leave. I will not always be held. I leave the one who loves me best. I hear and do not respond; I want and do not show that I do. I am kissed and do not kiss back. I cannot find peace in my solitary night walks. My soul wanders, stays inside a hiding place. Sometimes I love and cannot quit.

Show me my center. Keep me at rest in your lap; caress my soul. A pendulum swings from the center of my soul. Dear God, you are the center.

One life is not enough

I HAVE NINE *lives.*

Some of these may be spent already, but I do not keep count. I live as though all nine are still owed me. I will outlive my vets and the neighbors' dogs. I could do without shots and pills and the pokes and prods of the vet. But sometimes there's no getting out of it. And I try. Sometimes I don't swallow the pill when they push it in my mouth, but the taste is there—a bitter taste. They say I almost got run over. It may be true, but I don't remember such things. Even so, I have eight more lives. I will take more chances. Humans say, "You only go around once." I will go around nine times. Maybe more.

O GOD,

You give my soul long life. My soul began before I became the "me" I know. It will not quit when the "me" dies. I have been saved in daytime and in darkness. I live only for each day, and suddenly years have passed. I look at my years and see decades go by. I long for more days and nights, and you let me grow old. My birthdays come more and more quickly. My times grow shorter as I grow older. A long life is full of your wonders. I will live through more than nine lives. I will be saved more than nine times ninety. My soul will live forever with you. Dear God, there is no end to your life in me.

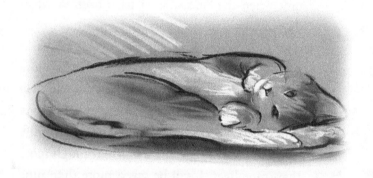

Let me snuggle

I NEED TO *snuggle.*

I demand it. I push and paw. I butt my head against them. This is who I am. I touch them; they touch me back. They pet me; I pet them back. They make me glad; I bless them. I purr; they feel the purr in themselves. The snuggle is in my eyes. I am at their feet; I leap up beside them. Close, close. I reach out on purpose as they pass by. I jump into their lap, not caring if I shed, not caring if their fine clothing turns white or black from my hair. Snuggling does not worry about being careful. I honor them with my snuggle. I indulge them by being close. My best spirit comes when I am held. But not too tight.

O GOD,

My soul has warm feelings. It needs holding and caressing. My soul will not be soul if it is left alone and untouched by others. It must touch and be touched. It must be held closely by you. My soul knows how to be held close—not too tightly, just right. My soul looks for you, for your life. We hold on together. My soul looks for others to hold. I snuggle. Intimacy can take many shapes and distances. But it is not careful of boundaries and cautions. O God, my soul must be close, must snuggle, must touch you and others to live. When far away, I need to be held. I want to feel your life. Close. Close.

Am I in your way?

I LIE IN *their way.*

They walk around me. I sleep, and they carefully step over my body. They do not harm me when I am most vulnerable. I lie in the open, where they come and go. I am a member of the family. I let them know when I am there. I put myself in their way: I sleep where they walk, lie where they would sit. I put myself under their feet, and they keep from harming me. I lie in their way so they will know I am here, so they will be careful of me. They know I trust them; they step over me.

O GOD,

My soul lies down in the way of those whom I trust. They know I am here; they step over me, around me—not on me. My soul is at peace in heavy traffic of friends. I will not lie in the way of those who would do me harm. I find places where my soul can rest and not be harmed. My friends know I am here. They know my need for rest; they know I need to be among them but at peace. They protect me. My soul finds rest in the open, in the presence of those who love me. I close my eyes where I will not be harmed. Dear God, notice me: I lie down in your presence, in your way. Dear God, I am here.

I choose what I want

I KNOW WHAT *I like.*

If a food isn't right, I won't eat it. When they change a brand, I can tell. If I like it, I will eat it; if I do not like it, it will stay in my bowl. My taste buds are demanding. Once I decide, I am stubborn. I am cat; I choose. They can't tell me where to walk or sit or play. I will choose. I cannot be pushed or pulled or coaxed or threatened. When I decide, they will know. Sometimes they wait and wait to see me make up my mind. I will never be led on a leash. I can be chased, but I will decide where to run, how far to climb, how long to stay away, and when to come back.

DEAR GOD,

I am willful. I choose what to like or dislike. My will is strong, stubborn. I want to decide where I will be and work and play. I want to choose my friends and enemies—where to go and not to go. Threats and coaxing will only make me more stubborn, surer that my way is right—even when it leads to disaster.

Inside my soul, a voice says *listen*. Inside, your spirit seeks to guide the direction of my will. My soul speaks to me of your presence, your promise. My soul is alive, growing, unfolding in me. And I cannot ignore it. Dear God, you made soul to be my self. Thank you.

The night is my friend

I SEE IN *the dark.*

My eyes open and let in light. There is no darkness too deep for me. I go out when the sun has set. I sleep by day; I prowl in the dark. I do not grow tired in the dark. My eyes are like the moon, and there are no clouds that hide my seeing. The night is when I am cat the most. They do not follow me into the night. They stay behind, wondering where I go, what I see, what I do. They sleep. I am alive in the night. I see in the dark.

O GOD,

My soul prowls in the night. In darkness, I see what I cannot see by light. My soul pierces darkness; the night cannot cloud its sight. When my day is clouded by darkness, by pain, by sorrow, by despair, my soul's eyes open and let in light. I see through clouds; I find stars and moon. I walk through shadows found only at night. My soul sees with eyes made for darkness. O God, you gave me a soul with night eyes. My soul can see distant light. Looking inward, I see into your beyond. My soul plays in the shadow of your wings. O God, my soul sees light on the other side of darkness.

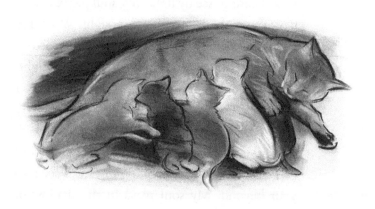

Don't forget my needs

I DEPEND ON *them.*

They think I rule the house. I jump up to places where I am not supposed to be. They look for paw marks on the table, hair on the sofa. They think I can do anything. They do not understand. I need their help—though I hate to admit this. I cannot turn doorknobs to go in and out at will. I cannot open cat food cans or pour milk from a carton. The doors are closed. The refrigerator is shut. The food is sealed in cans and bags. There is no live food to capture; the birdcage is locked. The toilet seat is down, and I thirst. I must lower myself to ask. They call me independent, but I depend on them. If they go away or forget me, I could die. My life depends on them.

DEAR GOD,

I depend on you. I cannot reach all I need. I cannot open clouds for rain, summon the morning sun or the moon by night. I cannot bring the end of day or form the mountains. I cannot call forth seasons in their order. The key to my life is hidden from me; the door to the future is locked. My soul must ask. I am born asking—for food, for comfort, to be held, for life. I am born needing love and trust, joy and family. I cannot find all I need or keep it. My soul reaches out, takes, licks the bowl clean, waits for more. I depend on you, O God. My soul looks to you—and a door is unlocked, food is opened, water poured, bread broken. There is help, so I ask.

I stare without blinking

I STARE.

I cannot hear my breath. I am a living statue—only looking, looking at, looking through. They cannot know what I see, if I breathe. My eyes stay wide open while I stare. I do not blink. I do not turn. I look straight ahead. What I see does not see me. I want it, will have it. The window separates me from it, from having it. I seize what I see with my eyes.

I am cat; I stare and do not blink. I know what I see. They watch me; only I know.

O GOD,

My soul stares. My soul sees without moving, not blinking, only watching, waiting, wishing. I take what I see in this silence—city, mountain, valley, friend, sunrise, nighttime. It is mine. It is yours. And there is more. Sometimes the eye of my soul stares inward, to what was, or to the distance, to what may come. My soul sees what I feel, want, know. I seize it in my staring: my mountain, my valley, my fear, my love, my story, my miracle. All comes from you, O God. When my soul stares, I feel awe.

Approach my things with care

I WILL CLAW, *fight, bite to defend my cat rights.*

I will protect myself and keep my things safe— for myself. I will strike, chase, stalk, scratch. I will make sounds of anger, power, threat. I will scream. I have named my territory; it is mine. Those who come to see me need permission. This is my room, my corner, my basket, my bowl, my yard. I will raise my back, make my hair stand up, scream my warnings. I will defend what is mine alone.

O GOD,

My soul will fight, defend, protect what is mine. My soul loves the life you have given me. I want my space, my time alone, my time with you, my holy place, my own room. I will not be destroyed, abandoned, lost. I will not let anything steal away my faith, my love, my honor, my home. My soul will scratch, howl, chase, risk—and defeat. I will not be beaten because you are strong within me. I may be hurt and wounded; I may bleed and suffer; I may grow weary and weak. But I will not lose what is mine, O God. I want your life in me.

Treats are welcome

I LOVE GIFTS, *a cat present.*

Fresh catnip will do for a start. Or a tiny ball that rolls fast or a toy they name mouse. Leftover turkey is also good. Sometimes they give me a collar with a bell and bow. And they smile proudly. I will allow this, though turkey is better. I will be pretty for them until I tire of the feel. Then I will scratch at my neck. When they talk softly and kindly to each other, that is a gift to me. I notice voice sounds. They rent a video on cats, read a cat book, and they look at me and smile. That is their gift. The best present is to sit very close to them when we are alone, hearing music, reading, being near. With my eyes shut, I feel them look at me with love. Being together is the gift.

DEAR GOD,

I like gifts: a ring, a sweater, a book, a framed picture, candy. A night out is a gift or a new toy, a gold bracelet, slippers. A bright sunrise, a soft breeze, a friend's call, being close to you—these bring joy. The best gift is the giving, the way you give to me, your generous spirit, your love. My soul loves the giving more than the tinted wrapping, more than sapphire, more than gold inside. What you give is homemade. You make what I need; you want it for me; you wrap it and give it to me. Giving is your great gift. See me: see how I want, take, open, wear, keep your gifts. Dear God, show me my gift-wrapped world.

I do not like changes

I NOTICE CHANGES.

When they change the furniture, I can tell. If an empty bag is left on the floor, I look inside. When there's a sandwich on the counter, I jump, look, sniff, investigate. When company comes, I examine them. I know if they've been near another cat even before they tell each other. If they move my sleeping basket, it takes me longer to get settled. I can tell when they're packing to leave. Then I hear the car coming in the driveway. When they change my brand of cat food, I know immediately. If they want to give me a pill, I can tell by the way they move, the way they look at me. I know it's time to hide. I notice when something is different. It slows me down, changes my plans. I am careful when something big changes.

O GOD,

My soul knows when seasons turn, when birds migrate, when skies turn dark or fill with snow. My soul knows when someone near me is hurting or bursting with pride. I can tell when a friend no longer cares for me. I can feel when something doesn't get said or is spoken without meaning. I know when something changes even when I cannot see. My soul knows when my life is changing. You know that I know. I have learned to live with changes, but they slow me down, make me look twice. I peek into something new on tiptoe. My soul plays hide and seek inside some secret paper bag. O God, you made my soul to know the difference between what was and what is.

Leave me alone

I NEED ALONE *time.*

I need to be all by myself, where I choose and when. I do not plan solitude in advance, but when it comes, it will be as long as I choose. I will decide. Right now you must leave me alone. You want to hold me, pet me, get me to play with string or a ball of paper. Not now.

I am not walking away because I don't love you. This is my little downtime. Perhaps I will nap, curl up in one place until being alone is done. Being alone is necessary; it is when I sort through cat things. The world will stop when I stop. Nothing will happen without my making it happen. You will have to wait for me. This is my timeout.

O GOD,

My soul needs solitude, being by itself with you, stillness to muse, coast, ponder in the heart. I schedule time alone—early morning alone, late at night alone. I withdraw to a secret place from time to time. I must build solitude into my life. You know my spirit and its needs: I may be moody, sad, tired, frustrated, or elated. I need to be with myself and apart from others. Solitude is a time for getting strength, letting the world go by, resting, not being in control, taking what is given. O God, your quiet is always here, your presence always near. Solitude is my exercise for peace, trust, cleansing, being myself. O God, there is so much in your quiet for the whole world to hear.

Don't laugh at me

I CAN HAVE *my feelings hurt.*

It can happen when I walk into a window by accident. I am embarrassed. I act like it didn't happen. If I slip on a waxed floor or lose my balance and miss a leap, I hope no one is looking. If I tip my milk bowl over, I pretend I did not do it or that I did it on purpose. I lick up the milk as though it's easier this way. I do not want their angry words; I do not like blame or shame.

Sometimes I need to tear through the house—a sudden dash across the room, a bounce off the wall, a leap onto a table. Then I am finished; I am elegant once more. This always surprises them, makes them point and laugh. I do not like this. Then I get cranky and sulk. I walk away. Cats are not to be laughed at. Cats have dignity.

DEAR GOD,

I am easily embarrassed. I do not like being laughed at. Sometimes I will bump into a thing that's right before my eyes, or forget a name I know by heart, or blunder when guests are watching. My soul likes to be right, to be admired, respected. I like being at my best. It is hard to forgive myself when I am clumsy or foolish or wrong. I am quick to blame others, to feel blamed, to show shame. You know this about me; you know how I am. I can strike back, run away, hide, sulk. I can act as though I did nothing wrong or that it is not my fault. O God, you know how I am. Teach me to laugh at myself. Teach me to love myself.

I will wait

I CAN WAIT.

They make me wait for things. I must wait while they decide. They decide what I need, what I want, what I will have. Sometimes I wait without looking. Sometimes I wait staring at them, looking up at them. I wait expecting something good—a tasty snack, dinner, a toy, a pat, a scratch under my neck, an open door. They surprise me. I receive what I did not know was in the refrigerator, on the counter, in the cupboard. I wait with hope. I wait as a cat must wait and wait and wait. Waiting is more than begging. When I wait, I expect, I long for, I count on them. I sit still and wait to be rewarded. Or I touch them, cry out, rub against them. I make sure they know I am there, waiting. They notice my waiting, and they are impressed.

O GOD,

I wait for you. Help me to wait believing. I wait for what I can never reach, never make, never deserve. I wait even for what I do not know is there. Waiting opens tomorrow, or now, or forever. Waiting keeps a horizon before my soul. Waiting grows inside me, unfolding, opening, expecting, receiving. I wait as a bud waits for the root to open the bloom. I wait for what was and will be. I wait to be sure of what is. Waiting is the joy of not yet having, not yet seeing, and learning to believe. My soul waits, learning to be sure of you. O God, my soul waits for what you promise is already here.

Curiosity will not kill me

I AM FILLED *with curiosity.*

Anything they are doing, I want to know about. I watch to see what they are making and how it will turn out and if I can help. I want to know what they are reading and how it feels beneath my paws. I wonder whom their phone call is from and if I can add my sounds to theirs.

My curiosity is strongest when I see them opening a box. I move in close. If I am close, they will notice me and show me. If they leave the room, I will investigate on my own. I want to be next to the box, on top of the box, inside the box. There is so much to see, to discover. I want to know what's next, who is here, what is there. They help me be curious. Curiosity keeps me alive, makes me a cat.

O GOD,

I am curious. I seek and knock; I wait and watch. I want to know what you are doing with my world, with my life—how it will turn out, if I can help. I examine what is far, what is near, what is done, what will come. I have so many questions; there is so much I do not understand. I must know. Finding out puts my soul in the middle of how I see you, hear you, believe you. My soul begs to comprehend. My soul searches in the dark, listens in the silence, is curious on the morning watch. O God, you made so much to watch, to discover, to care for, to hope for. Curiosity will not kill me; it will keep me alive.

Your love is welcome

HOLD ME.

Kiss me. Snuggle me. I am a cat. Talk to me softly in whispers. Stroke me with your fingertips and look into my face. Say my name. Repeat soothing words again and again. Ask me whatever you want. Tell me I am special, beautiful, elegant. Make your voice loving, caressing, admiring. Adore me. Be glad for me. Say how much I mean to you, what you will do for me. Stretch the truth; exaggerate your love. Show me your heart. Tell me who I am when I am good. Tell me I am very good. Say I am your best friend. Adore me. I am a cat.

DEAR GOD,

I need so much love. My soul wants to be held, reassured, admired, wanted. My soul will grow strong if it is held close, be quieted if it is kissed, become joyful if it is forgiven. I need your love. Caress my soul with your heart, with your voice, your promise, your grace. May I come to know you as my best friend, my soul friend. Dear God, you know how my soul was created in love and how it needs love to live—now and beyond this life. Your love is here without asking. My soul comes from you, and it breathes your love like air, feels your love like a touch, hears your love as a whisper. My soul is well when your love is its life.

The world is full of smells

I KNOW THROUGH *my nose.*

They hurry past me with leftover turkey; I knew they were coming two rooms away. I am awake, on my feet, following every step. My nose tells me this is something I like. I do not follow grapefruit or carrots unless I think there may be chicken or ham in the same bowl. I know fish through walls; its scent can wake me out of a deep sleep. I sniff the air and follow the smell. I come to the fish and expect them to share. Just a bit will do, though I will always ask for more. It isn't how much they give me because even a tiny bite will leave its smell on me. And then I have fish wherever I go. My world is a feast of smells. I wash my face and paws. I am satisfied.

DEAR GOD,

My soul knows the aroma of seasons. Your blossoms of spring are sweet-smelling; autumn leaves have a whiff of age and soft decay. Winter's cold sharpness carries the scent of wood fires. Each aroma wakens a time inside me and floods me with memories. Aromas of home stay within me. A smell, a taste, a whiff and suddenly my soul recalls meals and flowers and people— images of long ago. My soul is filled with aromas of places and times of year. Dear God, your April breeze quiets me with a fragrance of new bloom. The scent of candle flame can make my soul stretch, wake in awe, sing. My soul begs for a morsel of all that is sweet-smelling. You have filled the earth with incense; it is my home.

Let me in, let me out

I GET TO *change my mind.*

They let me out; I need to come in. I didn't see the dog out there. I didn't know it was raining. I smell food inside.

Now I want out. I need to see if the dog has left, if the rain has stopped. They won't give me any of the food. It is boring inside.

In and out, out and in, all day long. It's enough to keep a cat busy. They wouldn't let me in and out of here if they didn't want to. When I'm let in, I hope I can remember what I want; otherwise, I'll ask to go back out. I always need to ask them. I can't open the door myself.

O GOD,

My soul wants out. My soul must get away someplace new. I need space, air, adventure. When I am out, my soul wants back in. It longs for rest, warmth, the safety of home. O God, let me hear a voice I know, an aroma, a word of welcome.

Again my soul wants out, one more time to be gone, to get away, to seek what is new and exciting. Let me out, Lord. My soul needs a vacation, time off, a break.

O God, now I've been gone long enough, longer than I wanted. Let me back in. I need someone I know.

I want in; I want out. In and out. Be patient with me. Be with me—inside and out.

In an instant I am awake

I WAKE QUICKLY.

Even when I sleep soundly, one eye inside me is alert, peeking. In an instant, I wake from a sound sleep, and I am ready. I can be a night cat awake or a morning cat awake. Once awake, I am ready to do what I must in that moment. I can be wakened by a door opening, a waft of food, a motor, footsteps, any strange sound. While asleep, I am on call, on alert, on duty. I do not want to miss any sound that might affect me. If it is not important, I peek quickly and go back to sleep. If the sound is important, it becomes a bugle call: I am on my feet, ready to do my duty, ready to be cat. Sometimes I blink, stretch, yawn. I wake slowly, carefully. But when necessary, I can wake in the batting of an eye. I know when.

O GOD,

My soul is always on alert. When it seems deep in sleep, my soul can be wakened in a moment. While asleep my soul is resting and ready, at peace and alert. I can be wakened by sudden fright or delight. A wish or dream will wake me to test the wish, to live the dream. I can be wakened instantly, ready to fight, ready to rise and claim a promise. My soul is quick to react, faster than a word spoken, swifter than a feeling. When your alarm clock rings within me, my soul is wide awake. O God, you created my soul to wake quickly and seize life.

I am fierce, I am frightened

I AM FRIGHTENED.

Suddenly my eyes open wide; the hairs on my back and on my tail stand up. My ears pull back against my head. I am afraid, but I will look fierce. I am a warrior, even if afraid. I will prepare to defend myself, to defend my rights. Even if I choose not to fight, even if I choose to run, I first will make myself fierce—like a tiger or leopard. I will hiss and spit and snarl. I will growl like a lion. Look at me: I have grown bigger, more dangerous. I arch my back; my tail swings like a weapon. I am ready to do battle—or to run. I am a frightened cat. I am a dangerous cat. When the fear leaves me, I will be their cat again.

O GOD,

My soul knows fright. My soul changes size and shape when I am afraid. It becomes a force, a sword, a spear, a weapon. My soul is my shield and protection. It prepares to hold off the enemy—or to flee, if it must. My fright mixes with fierceness in my eyes, in my posture, my face, my words. I raise my voice; I make brave sounds, pretend to be stronger than I am. If I cannot fight and be strong, I will run. I must decide when it is wise to fight or to flee. My soul draws its courage and wisdom from you. I learn from my fear. You will guard me from evil, harm, and foe. You will teach me to fight or to flee.

Let me sleep, let me sleep

I AM CAT; *I sleep.*

I sleep long, short, deep, light. I know all ways to sleep. And I sleep often. I breathe slowly, quietly; my belly rises and falls with my breath. They watch me sleep when they are awake. They know I sleep often, sleep well. When it is time, I draw my body into a circle, put my head on my paws, shut one eye, two eyes, sleep. My body goes limp. I do not stir. They wonder how I can sleep so soon, so deep, so often. Awake, I lick my paws, my sides, my ears; then I turn and go back to sleep. I dream of stalking birds, leaping, climbing, chasing. My whiskers twitch; my body twitches with my dreams. They smile as they watch me sleep and dream. They want my world of sleep. My heart is quiet. I am warm; I am loved. There is no enemy. I am cat, and I sleep well.

DEAR GOD,

I long for sleep. My body rests, wakes, frets, tosses, slumbers, sleeps. Night is sometimes long, sometimes sleepless. My soul prays for rest. Day is done; work is finished. I close the shades, let go of my plans and cares. I think of you. I give you my day, my work, my thoughts, my cares. My soul stretches, yawns. I quit climbing mountains; I trust deep valleys; I forgive the enemy. I love. I sleep. My soul rests in the night. You have given me the gift of sleep. My rest is in your peace. Dear God, you made my soul to rest, to lie down in green pastures, beside still waters. You restore me in sleep and peace.

I choose my own space

I CHOOSE WHERE *I want to be.*

They give me a box with a towel; I choose a chair. They give me a chair; I choose a rug. I decide on my place to be. Also I like the chair at the end of the table. Its velvet cushion becomes my new place. They cannot sit in this chair while I lie there.

My basket with the plaid blanket has been moved. I want it back. I step in and out of the basket a hundred times a day. It must be placed by the window once more so I can look outdoors. I find another place—the sunny spot on the living room rug. I move across the rug with the afternoon sun. The sun is warming my spot on the rug. I will want the recliner at times too. They will not choose for me. I am a cat; I choose my own space.

DEAR GOD,

My soul chooses where it wants to be, where it needs to stay, where it feels at home. My blanket, my basket, my spot of sun, my velvet pillow, my cozy recliner. I have my own places, each suited for a mood, thought, dream, need. These are homes for my soul, places where I am always welcome. I go to my soul homes to lie down, receive love and strength, be renewed. My soul knows where to go when I need to reflect, be content, seek forgiveness, forgive. Dear God, you have made many homes for me, and in these places you fill my soul with love and warmth. You have made life so I may choose spaces for my soul.

Thank you and please

I AM GRATEFUL.

See me give thanks. I rub against their legs, purr, look into their faces, and thank. They know when I give thanks. My thanks are always followed by please. I can make them sound alike. If they won't give me more, I walk away as if satisfied, lick my paws, wash my face, and pretend it was a feast. But I am washing for the next course. I am ready in case more is coming. My giving thanks may be rewarded. I will give thanks, even if nothing more comes. A cat can be grateful. But they have been good to me; they will be good to me again. "Thank you" and "more, please." I am their cat; they are mine. I am thankful; I expect more.

OH GOD,

My soul is thankful. I cannot thank you enough for all there is for me. I wish I could thank more and ask less. I give thanks immediately, or later, or sometimes never. But I am thankful. When I give thanks, I belong. Thanking reminds me that you care about me, love me. Thanking shows me I have more than enough. When I thank, I also say *please*. Thank you for this; please keep it coming. O God, you have seated me at a very great table, a table that never goes empty. My soul gives thanks, for there is always more, so many second helpings. Dear God, there is room for others at that table. When I give thanks, I will pass it on; I will share.

Silence surrounds me

I WALK WITHOUT *making a sound.*

My paws move like fog; I hold my breath inside every step. I build silence around me when I walk. Soft sounds around me are stilled when I approach. I cannot hear myself move. Silence is inside me. I am at peace. My steps are careful; dry leaves become cotton beneath my paws. The place I am grows quiet. They cannot hear me. They do not know if I am near. The silence is my strength, my power. I will not be rushed. My feet glide and leap with grace, with purpose. I do not feel my motion. I am powered from within. I know silence. I am cat, walking still. There is no sound.

O GOD,

My soul is still. I breathe without seeming to take a breath. All around me is hushed. You fill my silence with peace and love. My soul grows quiet without trying. Inside, I am wide awake, alert. My soul floats on clouds. I walk in midair, my feet and head in heaven and on earth. I move on wings; I fly to you. All sound vanishes as I approach; nothing can enter my silence. Nothing but your still presence. I walk in silence, listening only for your voice, your peace. I am covered in silence. I am at rest. O God, my soul is covered with your peace. My soul is still.

2
God said, "Let there be Cat"

WHAT DO CATS have to do with God, spirit, prayer, creation, grace?

From childhood, I knew cats are special in God's life with us. God made Cat and said, "This is very good." Cat lovers know there is always more and more to learn from a cat.

The prayers in this section focus on the meaning of grace. Now, *grace* is a very large word and may come alive for you in these twenty-six prayers. While writing the prayers, my mind's eye sees the cat world and all creation huddled, playing and living under the great umbrella of grace. May you grow in God's creational images of grace.

Attributes of God are one way to know God's complete presence in the world and in our lives. Incarnation brings God all the way into the universe and to every part of nature, cat, forest, brook, raindrop, breath, relationship, emotion—every thought, word, and deed. God is embedded in all of life, and all creation is embedded in God. *Emmanuel* is an incarnate word; God is with us.

How easy to connect attitudes of God to attributes often evident inside a cat: "Look at me," "Care," "I know my place," "A higher being," "I tread lightly," "Good morning," "I believe," "Talk to me."

God said, "Let there be Cat. And it was so." For this, I am grateful. The attributes of Cat are what we, too, enjoy, feel, share, and depend on for life and well-being. Cats often remind me of how God has created you and me to live a life of grace. If you know a cat, look again.

It is my hope these cat psalms will please cat lovers and help them look at Cat in a spiritual way. Creating Cat was God's intent to make a world "very good."

In my eighty-one years, I do not remember when we did not have a special tree or rock or cat. Creation keeps the spirit of God close to earth and incarnate.

Pray these *cat psalms* with friends, family, children, parish, and those who are sick or shut in. God's Spirit will take you beyond these twenty-six prayers as you look at creation all around.

Herbert Brokering

Family

I AM CAT. I am a member of your family.
Once upon a time, I came to live here. Was it
by birth? Was I homeless? Did I appear at your
door? Did you buy me? It does not matter; I am
a member of the family. You call me by your
family name. I eat and play and sleep here. I
have my own bowl of food and my clean water
dish. Sometimes I eat right beside you; you
know how to set the rules. I am cat, and we are
family. You know where I nap and play and eat
and cuddle and sleep. I know all your rooms, for
I have visited them when you were not home.
You have told me which places are my own.
They are enough. When company comes, you
introduce me. They answer and notice me, for I
am your cat. We are a gracious family.

GOD,

You fill me with family grace. I am family with those who are homeless, with strangers, with neighbors, and with immigrants. I am at home with warring nations and political foes. Grace is my journey; I leave, and I stray. Grace is how I find my way home. I know the power and joy of belonging. I know the helplessness and pain of being cut off from others. See me share my table, divide my abundance, give my time, and extend my sense of household. Life is your gift to all. All share your one life and breath and spirit. You call us your children, and so we are. As I have a safe place on your earth, so may we all be family. God, at each dawn and dusk, I find this place and all the earth a home of grace.

Special

I AM CAT. I am special, for you say I am. You call me pretty and beautiful and gorgeous and treat me with respect; so it is true. I am flattered and will not make you stop. You brush me even if I do not need brushing. You make me special without my asking. You show me to your friends and smile; they take turns holding me. I hear you when you mention my name on the phone. You are glad at what they say. You look my way and smile. I cannot hear them, but you keep turning to see me while they talk. I can tell you are proud, so I am proud. My cat bed is homemade and matches your sofa. If I do not eat my food, then you ask me what I want. I do not answer; you leave and return with something special. Some say I cost more than I am worth. You do not believe them. You treat me as a prize. I am your cat; I am special.

GOD,

Your own grace is in me, for you have made me in your own image. You formed me in my mother and said I am very good; so I am. Some like my smile, some my eyes, my mind, my laugh; some like my spirit. How often my name is spoken for good. I am glad for those who know me, love me, and speak kindly of me. A banner was made when I was born; these are your words: "I have called you by my name." When I am down, when I do not seem to belong, then I am lifted up. I praise and thank you, for you are gracious. I am more special than a cat cuddled in a cotton napper. It is so; I, too, am gracious, a member of your place of grace. You look my way and smile.

Genes

I AM CAT. **I am full of possibilities.** There are rules and possibilities deep inside me, for I am cat. My potential is in my genes; this is my inheritance. This is my lineage. I had a strict upbringing that began when I was born, a kitten, with my mother, under my mother's tongue, under her paws. I can feel every kindness, every washing; I still hear my mother's voice coaching and warning me. I learned to fend for myself, to be cat in all ways. I learned to be quieter than fog, more still than breath. I can hear a mouse breathing from a distance. It is in my blood to listen. My mother did so; my father and my siblings did so. I know myself as cat, my kind of cat. Some of me is written in stone; some is written as in sand. I am cat—some of me is ageless; some is new. Grace is very old and is given.

GOD,

Your grace is old; your grace is new. You have known me from the foundation of the world, and yet I am like new each day. I have deep stories stored in old genes. Old grace is in me. My roots are alive; new twigs are budding. This is how you grow your grace. I am predictable as from old; I am new with surprise. The years of my life are in me; those who have held and fed and loved me have stayed in me. They are my story, begun in old times lived before me, a genetic pool from which I, too, drink. God, I have inherited a legacy of gifts that cannot be numbered. In me dwell codes and labels and markings that only you know. We Google, we research, we pray. We seek, and we find. Grace permeates all creation, deep within and still unfolding. Wherever we go, you are. Grace is truly present.

Time off

I AM CAT. I like time off, a break in the routine. A new hill to run, a new tree to climb, a different place to lie in the sun. To move around and find a nook I haven't stayed in for a while or ever. Give me a dark corner, the sunlight, a windowsill, under a porch, in the iris bed. Green leaves can be cool to lie in on a hot day. I need a mini vacation, a change of scenery, an evening stroll, a casual new friend, a confrontation, a risk, a scare, and a test to protect my rights. I need to see who lives next door, down the alley, and to know what is happening in the vacant building. I need time when no one touches me, or asks me to move, or runs a vacuum cleaner near me. I want time off where a corner is enough, when no one speaks to me, asks me to move, runs a sweeper near me, shouts to wake me. I am cat; give me some space. Grace is about personal space.

GOD,

All life is in motion. You have made us migrant, pilgrim, and curious seekers. Surprises are your great gift to us: a new neighbor, a sight we never saw, a song we never heard, a new vacation spot. We have not met all our neighbors or chosen all our friends, seen all our family, or visited all places we have promised each other. Jesus walked off into new places to find calm, to see clearer, to risk, to rest, and to embrace what is new. We, too, prepare for the surprise of grace, space to be on our own. We explore, reach out, dig, and reach places new. Grace is a wide circle in which to find a new place in the sun or a new nook on earth's great rug. I am not a cat, but I take off to be surprised. I am not afraid, for grace will follow me and then lead me home.

Special meal

I AM CAT. Sometimes I need a special meal, a treat. I have watched your special mealtimes. You light a candle; I purr. You laugh. There is not always a plain reason for the meal, but the smell of the meal is special. I am given seconds, thirds, a little more, something you know I like, a snack, a piece from your own plate. Food is special to me when you reach down to touch me as you give it, as though you prepared it for me. You surprise me and make me grand with food. The meal is made special by the sound of your voice, the way you say my name when you hand me a morsel, and the look in your eyes. You stand and watch me enjoy eating as though we are eating together. I smell the candle, and I am sure it is lit for us. I feel gracious. I am cat, and I need a special meal.

GOD,

Your house of grace is filled with special mealtimes. You are host for one sip of wine, a piece of bread broken, a blessing given. Heaven and earth are at one table. A morning drink with a friend and you are there. A casserole beside a candle and the gathering is your banquet in a potluck. Hot cider at an open fire on a wintry night and heaven is here. How special are meals when served in your household. Summertime and gardens are rich with harvest. Trees bow down to be picked; again and again you give us the first fruit of the season. One more meal is on the board; we gather to say grace. All food and drink is about grace. All creation eats at one table served by you, for you are in the world's one kitchen. O God, our food is about grace.

Mine

I AM CAT. My world is great for my size. Not everything I touch is mine; there is too much. I know what is mine. You have a chair you like best; I can tell. You sit at the same place when you eat. I need a place I know is for me, where you can look for me, pet me, talk to me. I need a place where my dish sits, my place. As a member of the family, I need a place that fits into this place we call home. I do not need to be chased, scolded, or frightened off. I do not like to be at the wrong dish. Let us decide together where my welcome space is. There are dishes I like, but they are yours. I know I am not allowed on the table or kitchen counter, though they smell good. I know all the places you say are mine, and I am a wealthy cat. You help me to know that my world is very great and good. This is where I hear you pray.

GOD,

So much is mine. You are generous, and we have plenty. More and more I want to know how to share your abundance. Skies and seasons and meadows and woods and gardens cannot be measured; they are plenteous. So much is mine to grow, to pick, to dig, to plant, to see, to view, to read, to sing, to take, and to give. My dish is full. I have enough. In this place of grace, I will share as you do. I will share my best bread, best drink, stories, walks, recipes, best thoughts, dreams, questions, and my best spirit. In this place of grace, what is mine is also ours. All life is graceful, so we all break one bread on the one altar of grace. We will help to satisfy the hunger of every living thing. God, your grace is very great for my size.

Chores

I AM CAT. I have chores. I roll over; you laugh. This is my work. I chase circles in the grass and leap for flying cattail seeds while you take pictures. Jumping is my chore. My work is to humor others, to make you proud, to see you laugh while I do cat works. I have my own kinds of gifts, which are my work: I keep you company, talk to you, listen, wake you, help you rest, calm you. It is easy to sleep near you, to lie at your feet and snuggle. I know some chores by heart, from birth. Some I am learning. You teach me to stay in my chair, go down stairs, and find where to sleep. It is easy for me to create a habit, fit into the family, and be dependable. I will take my place with you—let me know what you need; I will learn to please you. This is our place to live together, our part of the whole world. What I do I will do well. I am a full member of the family. I am responsible to you, for I am cat.

GOD,

I, too, have chores. Some I know by heart; these I was born to do. Some are new, which I am learning. There is work of grace to be done in the household of grace. Acts of mercy are tiny; some are great. The world needs caring. We do our work as work of grace: scrubbing, cooking, building, serving. Our good work is caring, hosting, saying goodbye, phoning, sending mail, looking in on a neighbor, checking on someone who is shut in, hearing a child's worry, enjoying a joke, wrapping a gift, preparing a party, sitting by a deathbed, singing a child to sleep. God, you give us chores of grace. My good works are how I played when little and still play, shared and still do, cared and cuddled and still do, looked into a face while listening and still do, hurried to help and still do. God, my chores are the gifts you have given me to do, and they are not done. I am not a cat and cannot jump and tumble, yet, O God, my soul can leap and make others be more gracious.

Play

I AM CAT. Where can I play? Do I get a table-top? Can I have a couch when I want? Can I have your bed when you are finished sleeping? What belongs to me? What is yours? Help me know so I will not feel wrong. When I romp, I want to make you laugh, feel calm, and be good-spirited. You have seen me walk with grace, sit and be admired. I roll over, and you stop talking and laugh. I want to make you proud when company comes. I can make a joke; I can be a clown. Where may I play? I will share a yard or room with others. I must play, for I am cat, and in me I want tall trees to climb, logs to claw, and earth to dig. In me, I know swamps, stumps, dusty paths, and creeks to run. Help me find places to be playful and to show the glad spirit in me. I am cat and need for us to play.

GOD,

You have made us playful. Life begins with toys, surprises, rolling, running, throwing, catching, pretending, imagining, dreaming, believing. Life is playful. We are easily made glad; we quickly laugh and tease and surprise each other. We play peekaboo behind chairs and fingers and doors. We see and don't see. We pretend to hide and are glad. Years pass and we still play. We see and do not see; we understand and do not understand; we trust and do not trust. We play to hide and to be found. We know the joy of finding someone hidden or lost. There is something in me I feel is playful: the way I tell stories, the kinds of questions I like, the twinkle in my eyes, my voice. Grace is playful. Grace knows every glad spirit.

Night out

I AM CAT. I need my night out. By myself
or with a friend, away, like a tiny vacation. A
place to go and there to know what it's like to
be cat. Off to be honest, silent, quiet, to ponder, risk, come what may. Nothing planned, a
retreat, meditation, prayer. A time and place to
look around, look again, with other cats. To see
what changed out there and in me, a refresher
course in Cat. A night for harmony, fitting it
all together, ready to be me, a complete cat. To
feel my strength, wit, agility, connections and to
admit my weakness, limits, boundaries. A little
space to help get ready to come back home and
stay forever. I need a time of grace to grow the
cat in me.

GOD,

People of faith go off to a quiet place to pray. You have sung songs of the heart with singers, psalmists, mourners, and prophets. You have raised up choirs and monasteries, where a spirit can retreat. Forests and meadows and night skies and vistas are silent. We stand in them, and you make us quiet. It is our night out, our day off, a vacation. Your grace heals, calms, quiets, ponders, meditates. Grace knows how we wander, that we risk, we stray, we are lost, we are called, and we are brought home. God, your grace frees me to ask, seek, and find what is new beyond and inside. Sometimes in dark times or on light days, give me a night out.

I like

I AM CAT. There is so much I can do. I like who I am. I am cat, and that is who I wish to be. It is enough. I am not like all cats, for there are cat choices. I learned early to like being cat with all my heart. I do what cats before me have always done, from their beginning. There is enough for me to do. They say I have nine lives; there is a lot of life in me. Watch me and see what I can do. You will learn to know what I like, and I will know what you like. Listen to me purr; you will know what I like. We are not all the same; look at me, love me, pet me, feed me, and you will know me. Show me what you like and what makes you glad. I purr. Life is good; it is enough. Show me you like who I am.

GOD,

I am full of life. My spirit overflows. Sometimes I go in all directions. My spirit expands, explodes, and bursts. I like who I am. I, too, chase circles and scramble tall trees and follow what I like. Then I come back, come down, and am still, and I know who I am. There is so much to do; so you have made my world. There are new places I go; each place asks me to stay. My life is full of invitations; I am not bored. I listen, I hear, I go. This is my life, and I like it. I listen to my head; I follow my heart. I go because it is not good to live alone. I go to feel their grace; I go to be graced. I will sacrifice; it may cost my life, yet I go. I know what I like. I live a full life. Then I purr, O God, for I know where I am. I am home, full, fulfilled. Grace fills me with a full life.

Stretch

I AM CAT. I stretch when I wake. I do not know about health clubs and workouts, but I have rules for being well. Doctors tell you to watch me wake and stretch when you get too busy. "Stretch like your cat," they say. Stretch. You come home from the hospital; I see you watch me. You stretch and yawn and roll your shoulders and bend your body like a willow. Like cats. You follow printed sheets; I follow a habit inside me I know from my beginning. I cannot read. I am cat; I stretch. I stretch, and I feel greater than myself. Watch me; stretch. Together we know the feeling, the gift of stretching. There is life in me waiting to wake up inside me. I stretch; I yawn. I am cat.

GOD,

I stretch. I am more than the length in me. I stretch; my muscles waken. Now I am greater; my body wakes inside. Morning has dawned. I yawn. Morning keeps waking. A new day, a day full of grace. I feel a song; I know the gift of stretching, singing into a new day. I stretch into the break of day and the end of day. I stretch, and I feel strength in me, a cool breath; a healing spirit rushes through me like a summer breeze. I see the cat stretch. The nurse tells me; the doctor tells me; I read it in fliers: stretch. The cat does it right. I watch the bird stretch. After a good rain, green grass seems to stretch. There is a time to sleep and a time to stretch. I stretch, and windows open in me. Dams break. Energy flows. Stress flees. In the simple act of stretching, your grace is at work. May nations when uptight, too tense, then see a cat and stretch, stretch. Stretching is an exercise of grace.

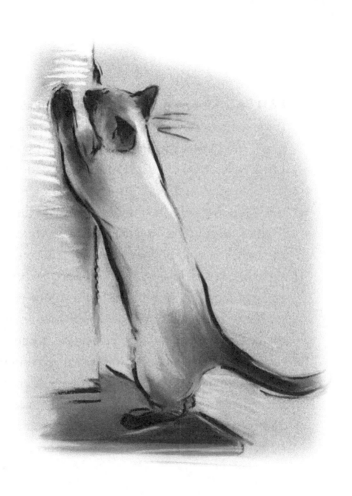

Diet

I AM CAT. I know my diet. If my food doesn't come out of a can or plastic bag, I know where to go, and I know my limit. I eat, I sleep, I wait, I run, I exercise, I climb, I eat; I rest, I ponder. I stretch, I plan, and I eat. There is an eating routine I follow; the plan is inside me. It was there from the beginning. I am tempted by foods that can only be found on food shelves. I join you at the table, at snack time, with leftovers, by begging through your kind spirit. I learn how you give in to me. I watch you at the microwave, at the refrigerator door and the cupboard. I know the sound of a paper sack. I smell what you bring in the shopping bag. I hear when a canister is opened; I can tell the snap of a cracker. I am cat, and there is a desire in me, a plan and routine for eating that I obey. We do this together.

GOD,

I sit to eat and say grace. We bless the whole table, the drinks, the salad and potatoes and fish and carrots and dessert. Let these gifts of grace be blessed. Cabbage, steak, broccoli, yams, tapioca pudding, we have it by your grace. Your earth and sun and rain grew the feast; farmers and migrants planted and picked the harvest. Merchants bought and sold it to me. The bounty is on the table, from the earth of Florida and Colorado and Chile and Mexico and California to the table. Ah, the route of grace. A meal of grace for health and strength. Ah, the power of aroma. Ah, the joy of a festive meal. Ah, the taste of a drink with a friend. Ah, the beauty of tomatoes and grapes on the vine. Ah, the taste of vintage wine. God, the groceries. The paper bags are full of first fruits. An offering sits on my table. Paper bags of food make my world of grace.

I sleep on it

I AM CAT. Sometimes I need time to decide, time to sleep on it. A good nap can make a big difference. A potential foe appears, and I am ready for battle. You are near with a gentle word, a soft voice, and two strokes across my back, a smile. The foe is not an enemy. I am not ready to play; I am ready for a nap. I do not choose the warfare. When I wake, I feel a friendlier world. I have slept off many battles I am glad were not waged. A nap is enough. I count to ten, go to a neutral corner, call timeout. I sleep on it to change my mind. A morning can bring a brand-new day, create a new feeling, and make me a new cat. I am cat. Give me time, a little time, to think it through. Grace needs time.

GOD,

Sometimes I sleep on it. Not long, forty minutes, ten minutes, one hour—a little time of grace. It is more than time; it is the privilege, the gift of a few minutes to ponder and to pray. A little time of grace. It is enough. Minutes make a difference. I am glad for a few minutes before going on. I am glad to catch my breath during a long decision. I am glad to close my eyes when people gather for worship and to see ahead. I am glad to stay seated for the postlude and make a promise. Sometimes I need to sleep in, sit in, and rest. I count to ten and then speak. God, in that tiny piece of time, I feel your grace. I will be more careful of my words. I will count to ten and not declare my war. I will count to ten, and I will return to my father's house. I count to ten, sleep in, take a nap: these are tiny gifts of grace, O God, and there are many more.

Make well

I AM CAT. I make well. I am no doctor, but I can heal. Let me sleep at your feet, and you will know the difference. I can slow a racing heart. I can quiet a heavy spirit. I can even rhythms of the heart that waken you. I am cat, and I heal. I have no medical credentials, but doctors will mention me to you. Ask them about cats. I notice when you hurt and move slow. I know the sound of a sickroom and will come to you on tiptoe. On the bed, I will make sure I should be there also. You lie still; I lie still. You stretch; I stretch. You open your eyes; I open my eyes. We stay close, careful, still. It is bright daylight; you sleep, and then I will sleep more. I hear your breath. You die; I mourn. I will hunt your spirit in every room. I will not let you leave me. Grace keeps me at your side.

GOD,

How easy it is for me to show compassion. How quickly I will walk on tiptoe, keep a room quiet, and make a spirit calm. How fast I serve someone who needs healing. God, you give me words to heal and to make well; you tell me when not to speak, how to whisper, and how to touch. You have made me a caring person to do what I have been taught to do. A cat has taught me, as have my father and aunt and grandmother and mother and nurse. I feel the healing hands and gentle paws of all who would make me well. How soon they come running with medicines and balloons, comforters and roses, and cool water and hot tea to a bedside. Grace is your credential of a healing spirit moving in and through us. A touch, a little oil, the laying on of hands, silence, a blessing, a massage, a hug, a right word—these make well. Grace is forever and ever.

Tease

I AM CAT. I have a sense of humor; I surprise; I tease. I have my way of making a joke. I smile, and I laugh as cat. I jump from my hiding place and attack your shoes; you jump. I did not hurt you; sometimes we laugh at the same time. I hear you. You bend down to pick me up; I dash away and escape. I look back and laugh. We laugh together. You dangle a toy above me, and I keep my eyes shut. I am peeking and waiting, preparing to tease. You think I am too tired; then I leap into the air and catch the toy, and you scream. I surprised you. This is my joke, my sense of humor. You say words like *cute* and *sweetheart*, and I feel your tone of voice; I know you like being teased. It is not the first time we have done this together. I tease you because we like the surprise and the laughter. If I hurt you, I did not mean to. Grace is sometimes a very good joke, a surprise, and a toy just out of reach.

GOD,

How did you make us to tease one another? We surprise each other with a turn of the eye, turn of a meaning, a gesture, and a laugh. How quickly we can be surprised. A bud on a tree makes us smile if the limb is covered with snow. You tease us with early sprigs of grass, a sudden flock of birds honking overhead, and a lawn of yellow chickadees rising in sudden flight. We tease and surprise children, so they tumble and hide and peek and do tricks while we run for cameras to capture moments of surprise. How playful is your grace; we stay your children all our years. We walk an old path, and it is like new. We bend to touch what we did not see before. Wind dances a leaf midair, and we stop to stare. God, we find your grace in toys and jokes and somersaults and surprise. Grace is fun, sometimes just out of reach, sometimes like a riddle or a profound joke.

Look at me

I AM CAT. Look at me when you talk. See me stare when I want you to help, to let me out, to give me dinner. I keep my eyes on you because I am cat, and cats must see your face. I notice your eyes, your smile, your look, the sound of your words. I can see from below if you are looking back or acting as if I am not there. You cannot hide your face from a cat. I will come close and tell you what I feel when you are not hearing, not feeling, not doing. I am cat, and I know your face, your hands and feet, your heart. Look at me so you know I am here. Grace will find the face.

GOD,

You do not hide your face from me, for I am yours. You see me from afar and from within. You see where I was and where I will be. Help me to see you seeing me so I feel how close we are in the dark, in a storm, in fear or grief, and when there is nothing I hear but silence. You see me with a soft wind, bowing willows, people in prayer, and angels who guard. Help me see your grace in the face and hands and faces lifted up in thanks and intercession. O God, open my eyes to see your eyes and to see the endless ways you look at me. Your grace means we see each other.

Satisfied

I AM CAT. I am easy to please. Sometimes I want just a crumb of a cookie, or I need one pat, one look, one word, one catnip toy. When I am satisfied, then I am best at being cat. I purr, snuggle, stay at your feet, stretch out on the rug. I will do as I please. I do not need expensive toys to make me glad. A string, walnut, paper bag, marble, twig, tree, treat. A spoonful, a few drops, a morsel will be enough. I need to feel you are there, that you know I am here. Being present is my greatest pleasure. I learn to know the sound of your voice to know my own name. I am not jealous. I am cat. I have enough; we all have enough together. Grace is plentiful; I am satisfied.

GOD,

I am satisfied. You need not give me more to please me. My world is full. I need time to open your gifts and share them. My wants are few. Sometimes my wants are meager and basic: a good chair, a loaf of bread, a bowl of soup, a drink, a candle, and a friend. There are times when I am easily pleased: a kind word, a touch, work, a wave, a walk, a robin, a train whistle, an apple. Each of these is a feast. I am satisfied. Life is full. Like the cat, one catnip toy is enough. One good word and I purr. A morsel, one smell of a bakery, one cluster of lilacs, one spring violet, a warbler, a bell, two children running, a family coming early to church and I am fulfilled. God, I am easy to please. I read one line in a song, and I feel satisfied. It is a gift to be simple. Grace is simple, and grace makes free.

Care

I AM CAT. I know when I am sick. I will not eat; I will not indulge. I hide and rest to save my strength. While I sleep and doze, I listen to my body; from my birth, I have nurtured my health. There is a lot a cat can do before calling 911. You are my 911 and my ambulance. You help when there is nothing more I can do. I am cat and know how to be well. I do not read health magazines or phone in sick. I was taught from the beginning to know myself. From birth, my mother said to me, "Know thyself." It is an old saying among cats. When I am sick, you offer me care. I do the same for you, for caring is an old rule of grace.

GOD,

I know my body. There is a lot I can do before calling 911. Growing well is also my work. Stretching upper body, lower body, bending, reaching, touching toes: I know these; I have heard and done them. It is up to me to care for myself and for others. God, you have filled me with medicines of wellness. In my mind, I see images of healing. In the psalms, you show me sickness and health, and I am comforted. You help me picture the look of growing well. I can see light at the end of a tunnel, a candle in the dark, a song in very still night. I know, and I obey. All nature declares your light and glory. Your mountains make me well. The cat gives me lessons in caring for each other and myself. I will learn from your whole creation. God, you give creation the power to care. This is your grace.

Washing

I AM CAT. I wash after eating. I wash when I have been in the rain. I wash when seeds and burrs cling to my fur. I am made to be clean. It is how I was taught when a kitten. My mother washed my face, behind my ears, myself. She cleaned me with strength when I was barely born, and her tongue was her strong washcloth. I did not hear the words *cleanliness is next to Godliness*, but they are written in my genes. When my paws have walked through mud, I will leave my prints on the floor and on a rug, wipe my feet clean with my tongue. It is the best I can do, and I will do so without a command. I am cat; I like clean feet. You like a clean floor. You wash me in scented soap and dry me with a clean towel. You are proud of me. You are gracious to me; I am clean. My mother is right: "Cleanliness is next to Godliness."

GOD,

When I am unclean, you wash me, and I am whiter than snow. I pray to be clean, and you show me how; this is your promise to me. In the beginning, I was washed, clean. With care, I was bathed. Again I was washed in a font. Every bath is a reminder of the font. How often I, too, have said: do not wash me. Then you washed me from head to foot; you washed me clean. I walked in the rain and stayed. I am washed. I washed in a river. It is my turn to be in the Jordan. I am washed. I bowed; I knelt. I was buried in sorrow; you lifted me up. I am washed. I read psalms, sang old hymns, confessed; I am washed. I ask that you create in me a clean heart; you renew a right spirit within me. Wash me with hyssop, and I will be whiter than snow. God, old grace makes me clean.

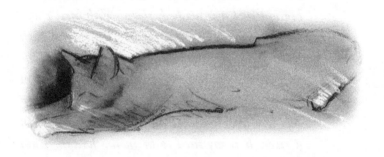

A higher being

I AM CAT. I follow you, sit by you, purr when you look at me; I look up to you. You keep me fed, make me safe, call me by my name, open the door, and let me in. You do what I cannot do. You are greater than I, and I do not clearly comprehend magnificence. You have earned my trust and loyalty. You give me what I cannot reach or do on my own. You open cans, pour milk, give me a blanket, open and close doors, and give me a name. Did you create the trees I climb, the rain I watch from the porch, the sun that warms me, and the snowflakes I chase? I did not make these, so surely you did. How did you create the squirrels I chase and the dog next door and a mouse? Who helped you make the hill I run and the warm rock I stretch out on in summer? How did you make the butterfly I can never catch and the bird taunting me from the high branch? You are taller than I, greater and higher. I need you to look up to.

GOD,

I am not the highest. You are, and I need a higher being. So I look up and see beyond myself. I give glory and feel myself lifted up, exalted. I need someone outside myself and family to give thanks to. Someone to esteem. I will stay in wonder and awe; I will marvel and bow and see beyond the end. I will trust and not comprehend, believe and commit myself. May I stay in the miracle of mystery and see every blade of grass, each bud, hear each song of bird, know each aroma of bread, and savor all raindrops as signs of your holiness. So may I obey you with speech and eyes and walk and will. Draw me to yourself through hope and dreams and faith. I will find you in my neighbor, where you show me your grace.

I know my place

I AM CAT. I know my place. I only do what I am able to do. I will do what you do if you teach me. I know many things to do by heart. I know I may not sit anyplace I choose; there are places forbidden, and I will need to be reminded. Not every bed is mine, and there are rooms I will never see. I am curious as I see you go in and shut the door and leave me standing. If you shut the door hard, I learn it is not my place. Being cat makes me even more curious. I try to honor your rules. Sometimes I feel it is our house, but it is clear I am a boarder or perhaps a visitor. No, really, I am a member of your family. I am cat and know where I belong and to whom.

GOD,

I belong. I am a member of a great people. I am not your whole body, but I am a member, a child, a citizen of your kingdom, your family. I cannot be all things, and not all gifts are mine. The days of life may not seem finished, and a lifetime may seem too brief. You give me my time and my place. There were others before me, and there are many yet to come. We all have our own time in your vineyard and our place at your one table. We pluck the harvest side by side; we pass the food to one another. I am one; this is enough for me to do. Show me the towel of Jesus, and I will show others your good grace.

I tread lightly

I AM CAT. Sometimes I go on tiptoe; I tread lightly. I can walk on thin ice and not break through. I can walk like the sound of mist, thick fog, a cloud in slow motion. My feet barely touch the earth when I walk in silence. Not a leaf stirs; I do not feel the stones beneath my paws. I walk as on cotton if I want, and my feet float. It is a habit I have from the beginning: to tread lightly, to be sure and not walk into a trap, for I, too, have predators. I know there are snares to catch me that I cannot untangle. I am cat; I tread lightly. Often I cannot hear myself, not even breathe, while I see and feel all around me, sensing. There is nothing I will not hear, but I do not hear my own heartbeat. This was taught to me long ago and has saved me; stay calm. Treading lightly has given me extra lives. By treading lightly, I may have not nine lives but twelve, for I am cat.

GOD,

You made life tender. Some days we walk as on thin ice, whisper, breathe lightly, and listen. The days are not alike; some times are tender. Your Word is old and changeless, and yet you are new. Some words march, some tread lightly, some are as silent as an evening breeze; some of your words unfold slowly like an early blossom. Grace senses. There are snares that we avoid, mines we walk around, and emergency rooms in which we are quiet, and there are the wounded with whom we are patient. There are feuds to which we only listen and do not speak. We, too, can be drawn into a trap or not. Grace sometimes treads firmly, sometimes like on soft paws, barefoot. Grace knows the textures, the feelings of hearts; grace wants not to bring harm or to be harmed. Grace is gracious.

Talk to me

I AM CAT. Talk to me. You do not need to
meow or change your voice. Talk to me as though
I am here with you, present with you, beside you.
Do not be silent as though I do not need your
words. Sometimes it is your turn to speak first, and
then I will be sure to answer. Your silence makes
me think you are busy, too busy. Silence can make
me wonder if it was something I took that was not
mine. I am cat; talk to me. I know what you mean.
I understand by how fast you speak, if you look my
way, touch me, how loud you talk, why you ask a
question. These are clear to me. A long silence is
hard to hear. Then I think thoughts that are not
true, and I feel feelings you do not have. I, too, like
facts, the truth. If you want to be alone, tell me; tell
me twice. Then I will join your silence. If you want
quiet, show me. You know how much of my life is
silence, resting, curling quiet on a pillow. I am cat;
every day talk to me, just you and me.

GOD,

You are a conversing God. You talk and listen; you watch and sing; we sing and watch; we listen and talk. You have said your words as music and prayer and prophecies and blessing. Your voice has been heard on mountains, in caves, on deserts, in sleep, in temples, in battle, in gardens. For long, you have spoken with us, your children. We have debated, obeyed, asked, agreed, bargained, and memorized your commands. Your voice is loud and very clear. Then you are so still; time passes; there is no voice of the Lord. You give me time; I ponder what you have already said. I remember what I have read and heard. Speak to me in person; speak through others in scripture, in my family, in this world now. You are not a silent God. Grace is a conversation.

Good morning

I AM CAT. I think it is time for us to get up. You do not need an alarm clock; you have me. I can wake you in person, however you want: with a purr, a lick, a nuzzle, walking on your body, breathing in your face. There are many ways to wake you. I have wakened and stretched, said my thanks, tiptoed, sat blinking; now it is time for all to waken, for I am wide awake, and there is a good day ahead. Birds are singing, the sun is high, I see a squirrel; the house is too quiet. Good morning. You need to eat; I cannot make you breakfast, but I can wake you, so I have. I would never wake you with the loud ring of the alarm. I wake you with my soft fur, purring, a joyful meow, and massaging your body with my paws. I am cat; good morning. O day full of grace.

GOD,

I wake in the morning again and again in so many good ways: rain against the window, sunshine in the face, still dark, thick fog all around, snow blowing, a waft of spring aroma through the open window. This is how I wake. Thank you. Come, O day full of grace. Sometimes I am awakened by a cat jumping on the bed, purring and pawing; sometimes the smell of coffee brewing, a door slam, the alarm, a child's voice, or just waking again on time. Thank you. Come, O day full of grace. How often I wake to a new day, a long journey, work, a holiday, a friend at the door, birds in a tree outside the window. Thank you. Come, O day full of grace. Awake, eyes wide open; time to dream, a heart full of hope, and a mind full of imagination, ready. Thank you. Come, O day full of grace. A thump on the bed, purring, pawing, breathing, a sure sign of life; breath, breath of God calling me through a cat. Get up; this is the day the Lord has made. Be glad in it. I am. I am awake. Grace means good morning.

I believe

I AM CAT. I believe. I do not need printed creeds; I do not recite presidential addresses or sing national anthems. I only believe. I believe in staring at a sunset, noticing the wind blowing, and focus my sight on weeping willows dancing on an evening breeze. My eyes will take a thousand photos of a sparrow on a high wire. I believe in the magnificence of walking alone under a full moon and seeing clouds make shadows on a midnight ground. I believe in chasing a leaf dancing in autumn, believing there is life in that red maple being. The toys I like best are around me. I wonder at the feel of sand, the slow motion of a snail, the speed of a hare, and the comfort of a familiar voice, the aroma of the same pillow. Some believe with all their heart. I am cat; I believe with all my senses. Grace believes.

GOD,

Your grace makes me a believer. When I believe, I am sure; trust and faith are your gifts to me. When I believe, I see and hear. When I believe, I will stare at sunsets, recite psalms, sing hymns, and stay to watch a weeping willow bud bloom and green and bow in a believer's dance. God, when I am bored with unbelief, send clouds and sparrow songs to help my believing. When I am tired of family, afraid of death, and lost in pity, help my unbelief. I, too, watch the sparrow on a high wire and feel my credo; I feel salvation when singing, "Nestling bird nor star in heaven / such a refuge e'er was given." I believe when I eat oatmeal, pack my children's lunch, smell a casserole, pour wine, light candles, pass the peace, rise to sing, study a stained-glass window. Your universe is filled with one grace. Any sign of grace will help my unbelief. God, you made me to believe, so I believe.

Routine

I AM CAT. Am I consistent? I like repetition, a routine. There are paths I follow by heart. My paths are marked like a map; my routines are predictable. You see me do them day after day, and you smile, as though I do not know. You follow me in the night and know my ways. There is a way I am used to. I do not like changing a habit I have begun. I have ways that work, and I know them. Routines fit me and all that is around me. I am cat, and I know my place. I do not like a door suddenly closed so I will lose my path. I know the schedule you keep; I know the bedroom, bathroom, kitchen, stove, refrigerator, table, sink. Each day we walk through our routines together in these places. I am cat; you know me by my habits. Depend on me. I do not live in a rut. I live in a way. I am cat. I have a way; you have a way. It is our way together.

GOD,

There is a way, a path I follow by heart. It is like a chart, a map in me. It is a guide by day and in the dark. The path is more than routine, more than a habit; I am a pilgrim, and I walk a traveled route. I see the marks and chapels and cathedrals and crosses of martyrs. The road is old and sometimes new. I follow this way with my heart and mind, and it fits my feet, my family, and my friends. I am on a faith walk, sometimes alone, often with many. We stop to talk and read and rest along the way. When I am tired, there is a bed; if sick, there is help. Some of the paths are too steep. God, you know the side roads marked closed. I try them. I am learning to know the way. I am glad to see the pilgrims. None is missing. Some are running; some are very slow, singing, dancing, praising. This is your way of grace.